Learning Sight Words Is Easy-Spanish!

by
Mary Rosenberg

50 Fun and Easy Reproducible Activities That Help Every Child Master the Top 100 High-Frequency Words

D1709261

SCHOLASTIC
PROFESSIONAL BOOKS

New York • Toronto • London • Auckland • Sydney
Mexico City • New Delhi • Hong Kong • Buenos Aires

Dedication

To Mom, Dad, and Elisabeth
for encouraging me to write.

Cover design by Jaime Lucero
Cover artwork by Sue Dennen
Interior artwork by Sue Dennen and Maxie Chambliss
Interior design by Grafica, Inc.
Spanish translation by Susana Pasternac

ISBN: 0-439-35533-8
Copyright © 2002 by Mary Rosenberg
All rights reserved.
Printed in the U.S.A.   4 5 6 7 8 9 10   40 08 07 06

Table of Contents

Introduction

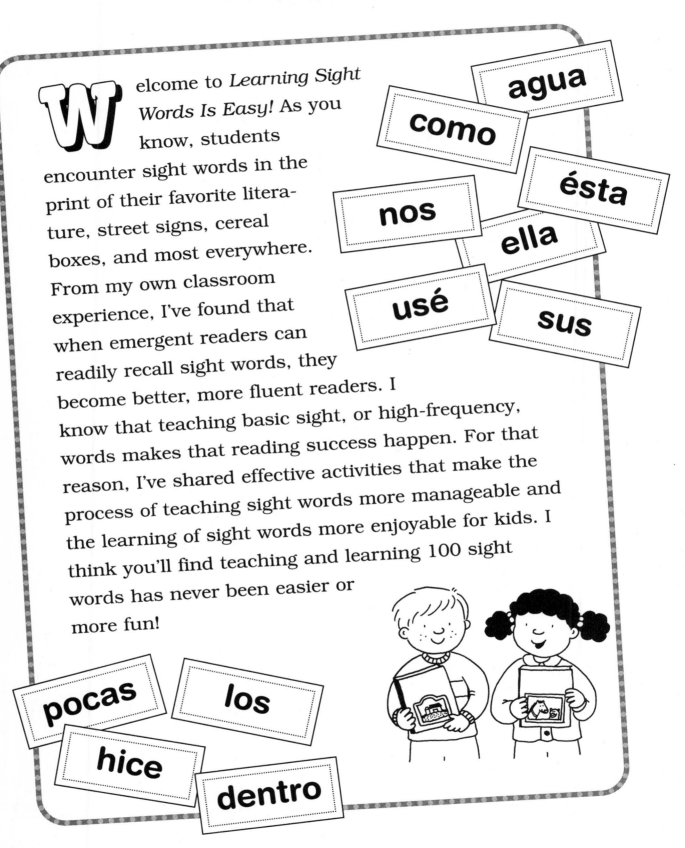

Welcome to *Learning Sight Words Is Easy!* As you know, students encounter sight words in the print of their favorite literature, street signs, cereal boxes, and most everywhere. From my own classroom experience, I've found that when emergent readers can readily recall sight words, they become better, more fluent readers. I know that teaching basic sight, or high-frequency, words makes that reading success happen. For that reason, I've shared effective activities that make the process of teaching sight words more manageable and the learning of sight words more enjoyable for kids. I think you'll find teaching and learning 100 sight words has never been easier or more fun!

agua

como

ésta

nos

ella

usé

sus

pocas

los

hice

dentro

How to Use This Book

Learning 100 Sight Words, Step by Step!

Use the grid below to locate specific words covered in this book. Please note that in order to make instruction more manageable, the 100 sight words have been divided into ten groups of ten. As you plan lessons, you may find the Suggested Sequence for Teaching on page 6 particularly helpful.

Words	Sight Words
1-10	el, ese, es, un, con, está, a, tu, en, sobre
11-20	este, como, la, su, están, para, arriba, abajo, hay, ellos
21-30	yo, tenía, se, por, tengo, esta, no, ni, estar, conmigo
31-40	estábamos, todos, estaban, allí, pero, también, él, una, qué, cuando
41-50	nos, cuál, de, los, dijo, te, mismo, al, me, junto
51-60	muchas, éstas, algunas, ellas, otras, afuera, las, ella, sus, mucho
61-70	has, dentro, parece, tiene, dos, más, le, hora, igual, lo
71-80	estoy, sin, quién, mi, primero, ahora, sé, mejor, antes, mis
81-90	sola, hice, usé, sólo, puedo, aquí, saber, si, sí, agua
91-100	palabras, sabes, mayoría, muy, largas, pocas, y, cortas, unos, murciélago

A Lesson Plan for Teaching 100 Sight Words

The sequence on page 6 has been provided to help you develop lesson plans. For each group of ten sight words, you'll find a mini-book and several companion activities. Begin teaching each set of ten sight words by reading the mini-book aloud; this will help students learn sight words within the context of a story. After you have read the mini-book, use the flexible companion activities to practice and reinforce sight-word learning. Of course, you should always feel free to develop alternate sequences for teaching to meet your specific needs.

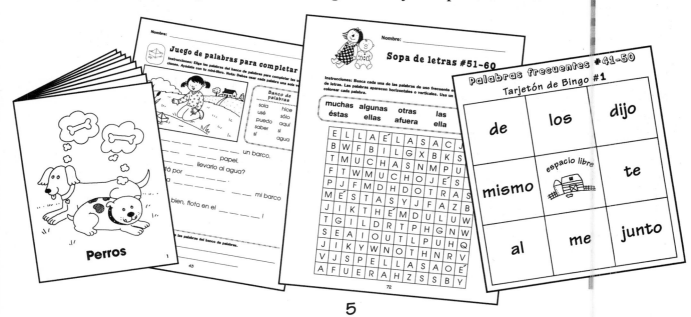

Teacher Tip!

Suggested Sequence for Teaching Each Set of Ten Words

- Mini-libros
- Juego de palabras para completar
- Hoja ¡Repasa, escribe, recuerda!
- Tarjetas divertidas
- Bingo de palabras
- Sopa de letras

What follows are easy how-to's for making each of these fun-filled activities work for your students.

Using the Mini-Books

Mini-books are a great way to introduce kids to sight words. Work with the class as a whole, engaging children in a discussion about the story.

- Show them the cover. Then ask your students to predict what might happen in the story.
- Read the mini-book aloud.
- Revisit each of the ten sight words that appear in the story.
- Encourage children to read through their mini-books on their own, building key reading strategies.
- Remember that mini-books may be used for shared reading and independent reading.

How to Make the Mini-Books:

- Cut along the dotted lines of the mini-book.

- Sequence pages by number.

- Staple the left edge of the pages, securing them in a typical book format.

- Invite kids to color the pictures in their books.

Teacher Tip!

Celebrate developing reading skills by storing mini-books in a place easily accessible to kids, a sort of mini-book library. Reading mini-books on a daily basis will help children build fluency and confidence as readers.

Using the Review, Write, Remember! Sheet

Use the Review, Write, Remember! Sheet on page 45 to reinforce correct spelling and usage of sight words.

- Begin by asking students to reread the sight words within the corresponding mini-book, reviewing sight words within the context of a story.

- Then invite students to write the word list down the left side of their Review, Write, Remember! Sheet.

- Encourage your students to say each sight word quietly to themselves, linking their oral vocabulary with sight-word learning and stimulating memory.

Using Fabulous Fill-ins

Help kids use sight words in the context of sentences with the Fabulous Fill-in reproducibles on pages 35–44. Some students may find it helpful to refer to the mini-book as they work, using the language of the mini-book as a guide.

- Invite students to use sight words to complete the appropriate Fabulous Fill-in, working in small groups, pairs, or independently.

- If you like, ask children to exchange papers to correct one another's work.

Using the Sight-Word Bingo Game

The reproducible Fun Flash Cards on pages 77–87 make great cue cards for Sight-Word Bingo. During play, students draw from the Fun Flash Cards deck and search for the matching sight word on their game board.

- Provide copies of the Fun Flash Cards and reproducible boards on pages 46–66 for your students.
- Supply children with game pieces such as buttons, dried beans, or Bingo chips.

Playing Bingo: Invite students to play Bingo at their desks singly, in pairs, small groups, or as a whole class. On pages 46 through 66 you'll find Bingo game boards for up to eight children to play cooperatively, with one winner. If more than eight children are involved in play, please be aware that there will be more than one winner. If you like, lessen the element of competition—Make a rule that the class hasn't collectively "won" until everyone has declared "Bingo!"

- To play, children will need to set up the game boards, game pieces, and Fun Flash Cards on a desktop or table. To begin the game, the "caller" picks a card from the flash card deck and turns it faceup. Then, he or she reads the word aloud to the other players.

- The "players" search their individual Bingo boards for the matching sight word. If there is a match, they need to place a game piece on the word.

- Encourage your students to continue the process until each of them reaches Bingo. Bingo is achieved when a vertical or horizontal row is completely covered with game pieces. If the players do not reach Bingo, then they need to reshuffle the flash cards, turn them facedown, and continue playing.

Teacher Tip!

Invite more advanced readers to participate with two or more Bingo game cards as an extra challenge.

Using the Word-Search Puzzles

The Word-Search Puzzles in this book will help build fluency by enabling kids to isolate sight words within text. You'll find the reproducible Word-Search Puzzles on pages 67–76 and the answer key on page 93.

- Discuss the ways in which words may appear in the puzzle—vertically and horizontally.

- Remind your students that there are ten sight words in each puzzle and no sight word appears more than once.

Using the Fun Flash Cards

The reproducible Fun Flash Cards on pages 77–87 can be used as traditional flash cards or for playing Sight Word Bingo, concentration, and more. If you like, place a few decks of laminated Fun Flash Cards in your language arts center. You may even find that their compact size makes them a perfect fit in pocket charts! However you plan to use them, you're sure to discover how Fun Flash Cards make teaching sight words easier.

Playing Concentration: First, copy two sets of the flash cards for several groups of three to four students. You may find it helpful to determine the small groups ahead of time, making the transition to groups faster and easier.

- Ask students to shuffle the flash cards and lay them on the table face-down in rows.
- Remind children to take turns turning over two cards at a time, looking for two words that match. When a student finds two words that match, he or she may take another turn.
- Invite kids to continue playing until every Fun Flash Card has been matched and removed from play.

Teacher Tips!

- Developing stories from Fun Flash Cards is a great way to put student reading skills into action. Invite your students to use flash cards as a word bank for story writing.

- Ask your students to read one Fun Flash Card as a "ticket" to go home at the end of the school day. Later in the school year, have each student spell a word orally before being dismissed from the classroom.

Using Read & Spell Flash Cards for Quick Evaluations

Use the Read & Spell Flash Cards reproducible on page 90 to learn how well your students are learning sight words. For one-on-one evaluations with your students, write the sight words your class is studying on a blank copy of the reproducible page. Then make copies for each member of the class and a copy for yourself. You'll need to cut your copy of the reproducible into flash cards. Now you're ready to evaluate your students. Find a quiet spot and invite a student to join you.

- Place one of your flash cards on the table and ask the student to identify the word.

- Flip the flash card over, facedown. Ask him or her to spell the sight word either orally or write it on a separate piece of paper.

- Note on the Read & Spell Flash Card sheet whether the child needs to focus on spelling or reading the sight word. Circle *R* on the flash card if the child needs to learn how to *read* the word. Circle *S* if the child needs to learn how to *spell* the word.

- After you have evaluated each of your students, make copies for your records. If you like, send one copy home with the Take-Home Note to Families so that parents can reinforce learning at home.

Using Read & Spell Flash Cards to Build Skills at Home

Since flash cards help students direct their focus on one word at a time, they're a terrific way to reinforce sight-word learning. Plus, the Read & Spell Flash Cards are easy to make and great for homework! Just have students follow the directions on the top of the Read & Spell Flash Cards reproducible on page 90. Then your students can toss the flash cards in a bag and practice reading most anywhere, including bus rides, plane trips, vacations—even the living room sofa!

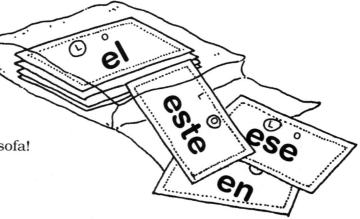

Formal Assessments

A few times a year, it's a good idea to perform formal assessments. (Three to four times a year works well for most teachers.) You're sure to find a routine that fits comfortably with your literacy program.

Using the Strategic Assessment Tool

To help determine how well your students are able to read sight words, use the Strategic Assessment Tool reproducible on page 88. Find a quiet place in the classroom where you can meet with students individually.

- Hold an index card under each word on the Strategic Assessment Tool. The index card helps to isolate the word on the page, making the task of identifying the sight word easier.
- Ask each student to identify the sight word. Check off each word that he or she reads correctly on the Strategic Assessment Tool.

Evaluating Sight-Word Spelling

Evaluating each student's ability to spell sight words provides you with valuable insight. If you like, assess spelling as a whole-class activity.

- Begin the process by providing each student with a piece of lined paper.
- Inform your students that you will be reading each sight word aloud twice, pausing for few moments between readings.
- Ask them to write the correct spelling of each sight word on their paper.
- After you have read the entire selected list of sight words, invite your students to look over their spelling.
- Evaluate your students' work.

Just Getting Started?

Ascertaining which words children know when they arrive in September or establishing the base line at the start of the school year is essential. When you have a base line assessment, you provide yourself with a point of reference. You then have a way of evaluating which sight words each child has learned.

Celebrate!: Use the reproducible Certificate of Achievement on page 92 to show your enthusiasm for student learning. Kids love to celebrate success.

Perros

Vocabulario de palabras

este	como	la
su	están	para
arriba	abajo	ellos
hay		

Otras palabras

hueso   árbol   hierba

2

Este es Fredo. Es un perro.

3

Fredo es blanco como la nieve.

4

Fredo está con <u>su</u> amigo.

5

<u>Están</u> buscando un hueso <u>para</u> comer.

6

Buscan <u>arriba</u> en el árbol, buscan <u>abajo</u> en la hierba.

7

<u>Ellos</u> no encontraron el hueso. No <u>hay</u> más.

8

El pájaro

Vocabulario de palabras

yo	tenía	se
por	tengo	esta
no	ni	estar
conmigo		

Otras palabras

jaula   pájaro

1

2

Yo <u>tenía</u> un pájaro. <u>Se</u> llamaba Pepe.

3

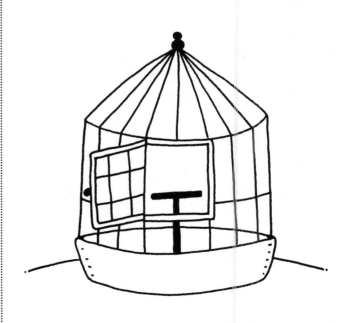

<u>Por</u> eso <u>tengo</u> <u>esta</u> jaula.

4

19

Pepe <u>tenía</u> <u>esta</u> jaula.

5

Las jaulas <u>se</u> compran en la tienda de mascotas.

6

Pepe <u>no</u> podía cantar <u>ni</u> hablar.

7

Sólo le gustaba <u>estar</u> <u>conmigo</u>.

8

20

La playa

1

Vocabulario de palabras

cuando	todos	estaban
allí	pero	una
también	él	qué
estábamos		

Otras palabras

playa   peces

pulpo   ballena

tiburón   estrella de mar

2

Pablo y yo <u>estábamos</u> en la playa.

3

<u>Todos</u> los peces <u>estaban</u> <u>allí</u>.

4

Vimos un pulpo, <u>pero</u> no vimos ballenas.

5

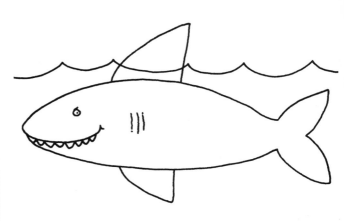

<u>También</u> vimos un tiburón.

6

<u>Él</u> y yo vimos a nuestra preferida. ¡Una estrella de mar!

7

¿<u>Qué</u> ves <u>cuando</u> vas a la playa?

8

22

La granja

1

2

A nosotros <u>nos</u> gusta leer libros sobre la granja.

3

—¿<u>Cuál</u> <u>de</u> <u>los</u> dos libros leeremos? —preguntó Ana.

4

—¿<u>Te</u> gusta este libro?
—preguntó Daniel.
—Sí —<u>dijo</u> Ana.

5

Ana y Daniel leen el <u>mismo</u> libro.

6

—<u>Me</u> gustaría ver una
vaca —<u>dijo</u> Daniel.

7

—Hay una granja <u>junto</u>
al camino —<u>dijo</u> Ana.

8

Muñecas

1

2

Rita tenía <u>muchas</u> muñecas como <u>éstas</u>.

3

<u>Algunas</u> de <u>ellas</u> eran grandes.

4

<u>Otras</u> eran pequeñas.

5

Rita las llevaba a pasear <u>afuera</u>.

6

Luego, <u>ella</u> jugaba con <u>las</u> muñecas.

7

Rita se divertía <u>mucho</u> con <u>sus</u> muñecas.

8

El reloj

1

2

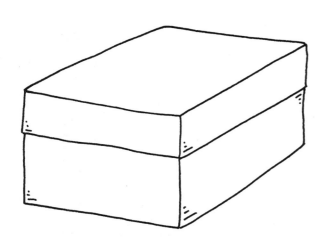

¿<u>Has</u> visto el reloj que Pedro puso <u>dentro</u> de la caja?

3

Su reloj se <u>parece</u> a un auto.

4

27

Tiene dos manecillas, ruedas y muchas cosas más.

5

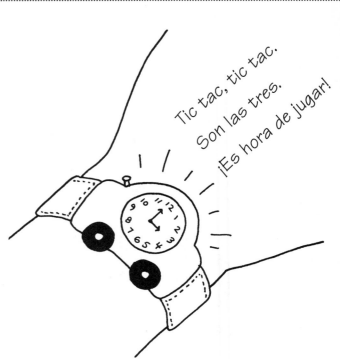

Tic tac, tic tac.
Son las tres.
¡Es hora de jugar!

También le dice la hora.

6

A María le gustaría tener un reloj igual.

7

¡Pedro se lo puede regalar!

8

La bicicleta

1

2

Estoy triste sin mi bicicleta.

3

¿Quién puede ayudarme a armar mi bicicleta?

4

<u>Primero</u>, pon las dos ruedas.

5

<u>Ahora</u>, pon el asiento.

6

<u>Sé</u> andar en bicicleta <u>mejor</u> que <u>antes</u>.

7

Les mostraré a <u>mis</u> amigos lo que puedo hacer <u>ahora</u>.

8

30

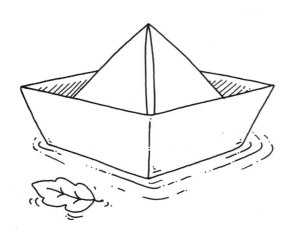

El barco

1

Vocabulario de palabras

sola	hice	sólo
usé	puedo	aquí
saber	si	sí
agua		

Otras palabras

barco

2

Yo <u>sola</u> <u>hice</u> un barco.

3

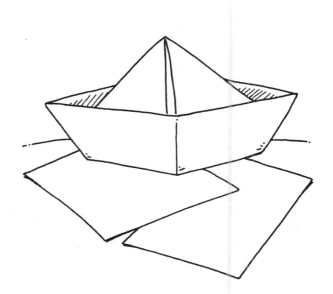

<u>Sólo</u> <u>usé</u> papel.

4

¿<u>Puedo</u> llevarlo al <u>agua</u>?

5

El <u>agua</u> está por <u>aquí</u>.

6

Ahora voy a <u>saber</u> <u>si</u> mi barco flota.

7

¡<u>Sí</u>, qué bien, flota en el <u>agua</u>!

8

sabes   palabras

mayoría   largas

muy   pocas

cortas   y

unos   murciélago

Palabras

1

Vocabulario de palabras

sabes   palabras   mayoría
largas   muy   pocas
cortas   y   unos
murciélago

2

mayoría

muy

¿Sabes leer estas
palabras?

3

largas

palabras

La mayoría de las
palabras son largas.

4

corta por la línea de puntos

pocas

cortas

Muy pocas palabras son cortas.

5

y

unos

"Y" es una palabra corta. "Unos" también.

6

murciélago

"Murciélago" es una palabra larga.

7

sabes palabras

mayoría largas

muy pocas

cortas y

unos murciélago

¿Puedes leer todas estas palabras?

8

Juego de palabras para completar #1

Instrucciones: Elige las palabras del banco de palabras para completar las oraciones. Ayúdate con tu mini-libro. **Nota: Debes usar cada palabra una sola vez.**

Banco de palabras	
el	ese
es	un
con	está
a	tu
en	sobre

1. ¿Ves ___ ___ ___ gato?

2. ___ ___ gato ___ ___ grande y con manchas.

3. Ese gato está ___ ___ ___ lado.

4. El ___ ___ ___ ___ está en ___ ___ canasto.

5. Está ___ ___ un canasto ___ ___ ___ un almohadón.

6. ___ ___ canasto con el gato ___ ___ ___ ___ ___ ___ ___ ___ ___ la cama.

Escribe una oración con algunas de las palabras del banco de palabras.

_____

_____

Nombre: _____

¡Juego de palabras para completar #2

Instrucciones: Elige las palabras del banco de palabras para completar las oraciones. Ayúdate con tu mini-libro. **Nota:** Debes usar cada palabra una sola vez.

Banco de palabras	
este	como
la	su
están	para
arriba	abajo
hay	ellos

1. ___ ___ ___ ___ es Fredo. Es un perro.

2. Fredo es blanco ___ ___ ___ ___   ___ ___ nieve.

3. Fredo está con ___ ___ amigo.

4. ___ ___ ___ ___ ___ buscando un hueso

   ___ ___ ___ ___ ___ comer.

5. Buscan ___ ___ ___ ___ ___ ___ , buscan

   ___ ___ ___ ___ ___ , y entre las hierba.

6. ___ ___ ___ ___ ___ no encontraron el hueso.

   No ___ ___ ___ más.

Escribe una oración con algunas de las palabras del banco de palabras.

_____

_____

Nombre: _____

Juego de palabras para completar #3

Instrucciones: Elige las palabras del banco de palabras para completar las oraciones. Ayúdate con tu mini-libro. Nota: Debes usar cada palabra una sola vez.

Banco de palabras
....

yo	tenía
se	por
tengo	esta
no	ni
estar	conmigo

1. ___ ___ ___ ___ ___ ___ ___ un pájaro. Su nombre era Pepe.

2. ___ ___ ___ eso ___ ___ ___ ___ ___ esta jaula.

3. Pepe tenía ___ ___ ___ ___ jaula.

4. Las jaulas ___ ___ compran en la tienda de mascotas.

5. Pepe ___ ___ podía cantar, ___ ___ hablar.

6. Sólo le gustaba ___ ___ ___ ___ ___ ___ ___ ___ ___ ___ ___ .

Escribe una oración con algunas de las palabras del banco de palabras.

_____

_____

Juego de palabras para completar #4

Instrucciones: Elige las palabras del banco de palabras para completar las
oraciones. Ayúdate con tu mini-libro. **Nota:** Debes usar cada palabra una sola vez.

Banco de palabras	
estábamos	todos
estaban	allí
pero	también
él	una
qué	cuando

1. Pablo y yo __ __ __ __ __ __ __ __ __
   en la playa.

2. __ __ __ __ __ los peces __ __ __ __ __ __ __
   __ __ __ __ .

3. Vimos un pulpo, __ __ __ __ no vimos ballenas.

4. __ __ __ __ __ __ __ __ vimos un tiburón.

5. __ __ y yo vimos a nuestra preferida, ¡__ __ __
   estrella de mar!

6. ¿__ __ __ ves __ __ __ __ __ __ vas a la playa?

Escribe una oración con algunas de las palabras del banco de palabras.

_____

_____

Juego de palabras para completar #5

Instrucciones: Elige las palabras del banco de palabras para completar las oraciones. Ayúdate con tu mini-libro. Nota: Debes usar cada palabra una sola vez.

Banco de palabras	
nos	cuál
de	los
dijo	te
mismo	al
me	junto

1. A nosotros ___ ___ ___ gusta leer libros sobre la granja.

2. —¿ ___ ___ ___ ___ ___ ___ ___ ___ ___ dos libros leeremos? —preguntó Ana.

3. —¿ ___ ___ gusta este libro? —preguntó Daniel. —Sí —dijo Ana.

4. Ana y Daniel leen el ___ ___ ___ ___ ___ libro.

5. — ___ ___ gustaría ver una vaca —dijo Daniel.

6. —Hay una granja ___ ___ ___ ___ ___ ___ ___ camino —dijo Ana.

Escribe una oración con algunas de las palabras del banco de palabras.

_____

_____

Nombre: _____

Juego de palabras para completar #6

Instrucciones: Elige las palabras del banco de palabras para completar las oraciones. Ayúdate con tu mini-libro. Nota: Debes usar cada palabra una sola vez.

Banco de palabras
....

muchas	éstas
algunas	ellas
otras	afuera
las	ella
sus	mucho

1. Rita tenía __ __ __ __ __ __ muñecas como __ __ __ __ __ .

2. __ __ __ __ __ __ __ __ de __ __ __ __ __ __ eran grandes.

3. __ __ __ __ __ __ eran pequeñas.

4. Rita las llevaba a pasear __ __ __ __ __ __ .

5. Luego, __ __ __ __ jugaba con __ __ __ muñecas.

6. ¡Rita se divertía __ __ __ __ __ con sus muñecas!

Escribe una oración con algunas de las palabras del banco de palabras.

_____

_____

40

Juego de palabras para completar #7

Instrucciones: Elige las palabras del banco de palabras para completar las oraciones. Ayúdate con tu mini-libro. Nota: Debes usar cada palabra una sola vez.

Banco de palabras	
has	dentro
parece	tiene
dos	más
le	hora
igual	lo

1. ¿ ___ ___ ___ visto el reloj que Pedro puso

   ___ ___ ___ ___ ___ de la caja?

2. Su reloj se ___ ___ ___ ___ ___ ___ a un auto.

3. ___ ___ ___ ___ ___ ___ ___ ___ manecillas, ruedas y

   muchas cosas ___ ___ ___ .

4. También ___ ___ dice la ___ ___ ___ ___ .

5. A María le gustaría tener un reloj ___ ___ ___ ___ ___ .

6. ¡Pedro se ___ ___ puede regalar!

Escribe una oración con algunas de las palabras del banco de palabras.

_____

_____

Juego de palabras para completar #8

Instrucciones: Elige las palabras del banco de palabras para completar las oraciones. Ayúdate con tu mini-libro. Nota: Debes usar cada palabra una sola vez.

Banco de palabras	
estoy	sin
quién	mi
primero	ahora
sé	mejor
antes	mis

1. __ __ __ __ __ triste __ __ __ mi bicicleta.

2. ¿ __ __ __ __ __ puede ayudarme a armar __ __ bicicleta?

3. __ __ __ __ __ __ __ __ , pon las dos ruedas.

4. __ __ __ __ __ , pon el asiento.

5. __ __ andar en bicicleta __ __ __ __ __ que __ __ __ __ __ .

6. Les mostraré a __ __ __ amigos lo que puedo hacer ahora.

Escribe una oración con algunas de las palabras del banco de palabras.

_____

_____

Juego de palabras para completar #9

Instrucciones: Elige las palabras del banco de palabras para completar las oraciones. Ayúdate con tu mini-libro. **Nota: Debes usar cada palabra una sola vez.**

Banco de palabras	
sola	hice
usé	sólo
puedo	aquí
saber	si
sí	agua

1. Yo __ __ __ __ __ __ __ __ __ un barco.

2. __ __ __ __ __ __ __ __ papel.

3. ¿ __ __ __ __ __ __ llevarlo al agua?

4. El agua está por __ __ __ __ .

5. Ahora, voy a __ __ __ __ __ __ __ __ mi barco flota.

6. ¡ __ __ , qué bien, flota en el __ __ __ __ !

Escribe una oración con algunas de las palabras del banco de palabras.

_____

_____

Nombre: _____

Juego de palabras para completar #10

Instrucciones: Elige las palabras del banco de palabras para completar las oraciones. Ayúdate con tu mini-libro. Nota: Debes usar cada palabra una sola vez.

muy   murciélago   sabes   palabras   cortas   largas   pocas   y   unos   mayoría

Banco de palabras	
palabras	sabes
mayoría	muy
largas	pocas
y	cortas
unos	murciélago

1. ¿__ __ __ __ __ leer estas palabras?

2. La __ __ __ __ __ __ __ de las palabras son __ __ __ __ __ __ .

3. __ __ __ __ __ __ __ __ __ palabras son __ __ __ __ __ __ .

4. "__" es una palabra corta. "__ __ __ __" también.

5. "__ __ __ __ __ __ __ __ __ __ __" es una palabra larga.

6. ¿Leíste todas estas __ __ __ __ __ __ __ __ __ ?

Escribe una oración con algunas de las palabras del banco de palabras.

_____

_____

¡Repasa, escribe, recuerda!

Palabras frecuentes

#_____ hasta _____.

Lee las historias de tus libritos nuevamente, repasa la ortografía y el uso de las diez palabras de uso frecuente que ahora estás estudiando. Escribe una vez la lista de palabras en la parte izquierda de la página. Lee de nuevo cada palabra para revisar la ortografía. Revisa tu trabajo.

Bingo de palabras #1-10

Instrucciones: Reproduce, lamina y corta cada tarjetón.

Palabras frecuentes #1-10
Tarjetón de Bingo #1

el	un	con
está	espacio libre	a
tu	en	sobre

Palabras frecuentes #1-10
Tarjetón de Bingo #2

sobre	es	con
está	espacio libre	a
tu	en	ese

Palabras frecuentes #1-10
Tarjetón de Bingo #3

el	ese	es
un	espacio libre	a
tu	sobre	en

Palabras frecuentes #1-10
Tarjetón de Bingo #4

ese	el	es
está	espacio libre	con
un	en	sobre

46

Bingo de palabras #1-10

Instrucciones: Reproduce, lamina y corta cada tarjetón.

Tarjetón de Bingo #5

un	está	con
ese	*espacio libre*	el
es	a	tu

Tarjetón de Bingo #6

ese	el	un
con	*espacio libre*	tu
en	sobre	a

Tarjetón de Bingo #7

el	es	ese
un	*espacio libre*	está
sobre	tu	a

Tarjetón de Bingo #8

sobre	tu	a
está	*espacio libre*	un
con	el	es

47

Bingo de palabras #11-20

Instrucciones: Reproduce, lamina y corta cada tarjetón.

Palabras frecuentes #11-20
Tarjetón de Bingo #1

la	su	están
para	*espacio libre*	arriba
hay	abajo	ellos

Palabras frecuentes #11-20
Tarjetón de Bingo #2

este	como	están
para	*espacio libre*	abajo
ellos	arriba	hay

Palabras frecuentes #11-20
Tarjetón de Bingo #3

este	como	abajo
su	*espacio libre*	hay
arriba	la	ellos

Palabras frecuentes #11-20
Tarjetón de Bingo #4

como	la	este
están	*espacio libre*	su
para	ellos	abajo

Bingo de palabras #11-20

Instrucciones: Reproduce, lamina y corta cada tarjetón.

Palabras frecuentes #11-20
Tarjetón de Bingo #5

arriba	este	como
la	*espacio libre*	su
están	para	hay

Palabras frecuentes #11-20
Tarjetón de Bingo #6

abajo	ellos	hay
para	*espacio libre*	su
la	como	este

Palabras frecuentes #11-20
Tarjetón de Bingo #7

este	la	su
están	*espacio libre*	para
hay	arriba	ellos

Palabras frecuentes #11-20
Tarjetón de Bingo #8

su	están	hay
como	*espacio libre*	la
arriba	ellos	abajo

49

Bingo de palabras #21-30

Instrucciones: Reproduce, lamina y corta cada tarjetón.

Palabras frecuentes #21-30

Tarjetón de Bingo #1

por	se	tengo
conmigo	*espacio libre*	no
ni	estar	esta

Palabras frecuentes #21-30

Tarjetón de Bingo #2

yo	tenía	esta
conmigo	*espacio libre*	no
tengo	estar	ni

Palabras frecuentes #21-30

Tarjetón de Bingo #3

por	tenía	yo
se	*espacio libre*	no
ni	estar	tengo

Palabras frecuentes #21-30

Tarjetón de Bingo #4

se	tengo	conmigo
esta	*espacio libre*	tenía
por	estar	yo

Bingo de palabras #21-30

Instrucciones: Reproduce, lamina y corta cada tarjetón.

Palabras frecuentes #21-30
Tarjetón de Bingo #5

yo	por	tenía
se	*espacio libre*	tengo
no	conmigo	ni

Palabras frecuentes #21-30
Tarjetón de Bingo #6

tenía	esta	por
se	*espacio libre*	tengo
no	ni	yo

Palabras frecuentes #21-30
Tarjetón de Bingo #7

por	yo	se
esta	*espacio libre*	no
ni	estar	conmigo

Palabras frecuentes #21-30
Tarjetón de Bingo #8

no	ni	estar
se	*espacio libre*	tengo
yo	por	tenía

Bingo de palabras #31-40

Instrucciones: Reproduce, lamina y corta cada tarjetón.

Palabras frecuentes #31-40
Tarjetón de Bingo #1

allí	estaban	pero
él	*espacio libre*	qué
también	una	cuando

Palabras frecuentes #31-40
Tarjetón de Bingo #2

estábamos	todos	pero
también	*espacio libre*	qué
él	una	cuando

Palabras frecuentes #31-40
Tarjetón de Bingo #3

todos	estábamos	cuando
estaban	*espacio libre*	qué
también	una	allí

Palabras frecuentes #31-40
Tarjetón de Bingo #4

allí	todos	estábamos
estaban	*espacio libre*	pero
él	una	cuando

Bingo de palabras #31-40

Instrucciones: Reproduce, lamina y corta cada tarjetón.

Palabras frecuentes #31-40
Tarjetón de Bingo #5

también	qué	él
pero	espacio libre	estaban
allí	todos	estábamos

Palabras frecuentes #31-40
Tarjetón de Bingo #6

todos	una	estaban
pero	espacio libre	él
qué	allí	cuando

Palabras frecuentes #31-40
Tarjetón de Bingo #7

estábamos	todos	él
pero	espacio libre	allí
qué	una	cuando

Palabras frecuentes #31-40
Tarjetón de Bingo #8

todos	pero	allí
él	espacio libre	también
una	cuando	qué

Bingo de palabras #41-50

Instrucciones: Reproduce, lamina y corta cada tarjetón.

corta por la línea más gruesa

Palabras frecuentes #41-50
Tarjetón de Bingo #1

de	los	dijo
mismo	espacio libre	te
al	me	junto

Palabras frecuentes #41-50
Tarjetón de Bingo #2

nos	cuál	dijo
mismo	espacio libre	junto
al	me	te

Palabras frecuentes #41-50
Tarjetón de Bingo #3

de	nos	cuál
los	espacio libre	te
al	me	junto

Palabras frecuentes #41-50
Tarjetón de Bingo #4

cuál	nos	mismo
dijo	espacio libre	los
de	junto	me

54

Bingo de palabras #41-50

Instrucciones: Reproduce, lamina y corta cada tarjetón.

Tarjetón de Bingo #5

mismo	de	al
dijo	*espacio libre*	los
nos	cuál	te

Tarjetón de Bingo #6

dijo	los	de
nos	*espacio libre*	te
al	me	junto

Tarjetón de Bingo #7

de	cuál	los
dijo	*espacio libre*	mismo
al	me	te

Tarjetón de Bingo #8

junto	te	al
mismo	*espacio libre*	dijo
de	cuál	nos

Bingo de palabras #51-60

Instrucciones: Reproduce, lamina y corta cada tarjetón.

Palabras frecuentes #51-60
Tarjetón de Bingo #1

afuera	ella	algunas
mucho	*espacio libre*	ellas
otras	las	sus

Palabras frecuentes #51-60
Tarjetón de Bingo #2

muchas	éstas	algunas
ellas	*espacio libre*	mucho
sus	las	otras

Palabras frecuentes #51-60
Tarjetón de Bingo #3

éstas	ellas	afuera
ella	*espacio libre*	muchas
otras	sus	las

Palabras frecuentes #51-60
Tarjetón de Bingo #4

sus	las	mucho
algunas	*espacio libre*	ella
afuera	muchas	éstas

corta por la línea más gruesa

Bingo de palabras #51-60

Instrucciones: Reproduce, lamina y corta cada tarjetón.

Tarjetón de Bingo #5

otras	ellas	mucho
ella	*espacio libre*	afuera
algunas	muchas	éstas

Tarjetón de Bingo #6

ellas	otras	las
sus	*espacio libre*	mucho
éstas	muchas	ella

Tarjetón de Bingo #7

éstas	afuera	ella
algunas	*espacio libre*	mucho
ellas	otras	sus

Tarjetón de Bingo #8

ella	mucho	sus
las	*espacio libre*	otras
ellas	muchas	éstas

Bingo de palabras #61-70

Instrucciones: Reproduce, lamina y corta cada tarjetón.

corta por la linea más gruesa

parece	tiene	dos
más	*espacio libre*	le
dentro	igual	hora

has	dentro	dos
le	*espacio libre*	más
lo	igual	hora

parece	dentro	has
tiene	*espacio libre*	hora
le	lo	igual

lo	igual	dentro
dos	*espacio libre*	tiene
parece	más	has

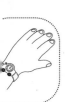

Bingo de palabras #61-70

Instrucciones: Reproduce, lamina y corta cada tarjetón.

le	hora	más
dentro	*espacio libre*	tiene
has	parece	dos

parece	has	tiene
dos	*espacio libre*	más
le	hora	lo

dos	más	le
hora	*espacio libre*	igual
lo	has	dentro

más	dos	tiene
dentro	*espacio libre*	parece
le	lo	igual

Bingo de palabras #71-80

Instrucciones: Reproduce, lamina y corta cada tarjetón.

Palabras frecuentes #71-80
Tarjetón de Bingo #1

quién	mi	primero
sin	espacio libre	ahora
sé	antes	mis

Palabras frecuentes #71-80
Tarjetón de Bingo #2

estoy	mejor	sin
primero	espacio libre	sé
ahora	mis	antes

Palabras frecuentes #71-80
Tarjetón de Bingo #3

quién	mejor	estoy
mi	espacio libre	ahora
sé	antes	mis

Palabras frecuentes #71-80
Tarjetón de Bingo #4

mi	primero	sin
estoy	espacio libre	mejor
quién	mis	antes

60

Bingo de palabras #71-80

Instrucciones: Reproduce, lamina y corta cada tarjetón.

Palabras frecuentes #71-80
Tarjetón de Bingo #5

ahora	sé	sin
primero	espacio libre BICICLETA	mi
quién	mejor	estoy

Palabras frecuentes #71-80
Tarjetón de Bingo #6

mi	sin	ahora
sé	espacio libre BICICLETA	antes
mis	estoy	quién

Palabras frecuentes #71-80
Tarjetón de Bingo #7

mejor	quién	mi
mis	espacio libre BICICLETA	sin
antes	primero	sé

Palabras frecuentes #71-80
Tarjetón de Bingo #8

mi	mejor	antes
ahora	espacio libre BICICLETA	mis
sé	estoy	sin

Bingo de palabras #81-90

Instrucciones: Reproduce, lamina y corta cada tarjetón.

corta por la línea más gruesa

Tarjetón de Bingo #1

usé	sólo	puedo
aquí	*espacio libre*	saber
si	agua	sí

Tarjetón de Bingo #2

saber	si	agua
sí	*espacio libre*	aquí
puedo	sola	hice

Tarjetón de Bingo #3

sola	hice	usé
sí	*espacio libre*	saber
sólo	agua	si

Tarjetón de Bingo #4

usé	sola	hice
puedo	*espacio libre*	sólo
aquí	sí	agua

Bingo de palabras #81-90

Instrucciones: Reproduce, lamina y corta cada tarjetón.

Palabras frecuentes #81-90
Tarjetón de Bingo #5

aquí	sólo	puedo
hice	*espacio libre*	usé
sola	saber	si

Palabras frecuentes #81-90
Tarjetón de Bingo #6

agua	saber	aquí
si	*espacio libre*	sólo
usé	hice	sola

Palabras frecuentes #81-90
Tarjetón de Bingo #7

sola	puedo	hice
aquí	*espacio libre*	sí
saber	si	agua

Palabras frecuentes #81-90
Tarjetón de Bingo #8

usé	agua	sí
si	*espacio libre*	hice
sólo	puedo	sola

Bingo de palabras #91-100

Instrucciones: Reproduce, lamina y corta cada tarjetón.

Palabras frecuentes #91-100
Tarjetón de Bingo #1

mayoría	muy	largas
murciélago	*espacio libre*	y
cortas	unos	pocas

Palabras frecuentes #91-100
Tarjetón de Bingo #2

palabras	sabes	largas
y	*espacio libre*	murciélago
pocas	cortas	unos

Palabras frecuentes #91-100
Tarjetón de Bingo #3

mayoría	muy	y
sabes	*espacio libre*	cortas
pocas	palabras	unos

Palabras frecuentes #91-100
Tarjetón de Bingo #4

sabes	palabras	mayoría
muy	*espacio libre*	murciélago
unos	pocas	largas

Bingo de palabras #91-100

Instrucciones: Reproduce, lamina y corta cada tarjetón.

Palabras frecuentes #91-100
Tarjetón de Bingo #5

muy	murciélago	largas
palabras	*espacio libre*	mayoría
sabes	y	cortas

Palabras frecuentes #91-100
Tarjetón de Bingo #6

sabes	mayoría	muy
largas	*espacio libre*	cortas
y	unos	pocas

Palabras frecuentes #91-100
Tarjetón de Bingo #7

pocas	unos	y
cortas	*espacio libre*	muy
sabes	palabras	largas

Palabras frecuentes #91-100
Tarjetón de Bingo #8

unos	cortas	pocas
y	*espacio libre*	muy
murciélago	sabes	mayoría

Bingo de palabras (en blanco)

Instrucciones: Reproduce, lamina y corta cada tarjetón.

Palabras frecuentes
Tarjetón de Bingo

	espacio libre	

Palabras frecuentes
Tarjetón de Bingo

	espacio libre	

Palabras frecuentes
Tarjetón de Bingo

	espacio libre	

Palabras frecuentes
Tarjetón de Bingo

	espacio libre	

Sopa de letras #1-10

Instrucciones: Busca cada una de las palabras de uso frecuente escondidas en esta sopa de letras. Las palabras aparecen horizontales o verticales. Usa un lápiz de color para colorear cada palabra.

el	es	con	a	en
ese	un	está	tu	sobre

Á	L	S	O	B	R	E	Y	R	H	E	S
O	Y	O	U	S	G	O	M	Y	R	T	Q
L	U	T	N	F	Q	X	P	X	N	M	L
X	Y	T	P	E	G	F	S	Y	Á	B	Q
Á	O	O	R	S	Z	D	P	B	E	R	E
U	Q	K	L	E	R	E	M	N	U	X	N
D	I	Z	J	D	O	F	V	T	X	Q	Q
N	T	T	Y	M	J	C	X	V	L	C	W
T	Á	S	B	K	Y	O	E	F	D	P	D
Q	P	R	T	A	N	N	X	T	R	Á	T
I	N	R	H	V	J	Z	U	F	E	L	E
E	S	T	Á	J	T	U	E	H	D	F	Z

Sopa de letras #11-20

Instrucciones: Busca cada una de las palabras de uso frecuente escondidas en esta sopa de letras. Las palabras aparecen horizontales o verticales. Usa un lápiz de color para colorear cada palabra.

este	la	están	arriba	hay
como	su	para	abajo	ellos

E	S	T	Á	N	Y	C	D	O	U	X	H
Á	U	W	V	K	O	R	L	P	A	R	A
P	H	D	F	P	M	J	F	M	R	Y	Y
Z	G	O	N	N	G	X	M	I	N	O	I
J	E	L	L	O	S	U	Q	R	H	T	B
S	W	T	H	E	E	L	L	M	S	V	Q
H	E	O	P	S	H	A	R	R	I	B	A
W	E	L	U	T	L	B	N	H	B	C	B
N	Q	B	J	E	W	W	Á	S	I	G	A
B	Z	E	F	O	R	B	F	H	Á	S	J
L	C	G	D	F	O	E	Q	C	L	T	O
A	I	T	H	B	C	O	M	O	S	W	O

Sopa de letras #21-30

Instrucciones: Busca cada una de las palabras de uso frecuente escondidas en esta sopa de letras. Las palabras aparecen horizontales o verticales. Usa un lápiz de color para colorear cada palabra.

yo	se	tengo	no	estar
tenía	por	esta	ni	conmigo

G	E	S	T	A	R	Z	H	E	J	H	Y
H	A	V	E	G	G	Q	Í	P	H	S	Í
S	A	S	Q	D	S	J	N	W	P	M	A
N	O	J	H	A	Y	T	E	N	G	O	S
H	U	V	S	H	O	K	C	K	C	R	E
R	R	T	O	N	E	X	T	O	G	C	G
T	Z	M	F	I	P	J	M	Z	J	O	F
T	L	Í	S	Q	O	D	Y	L	Q	N	R
T	E	N	Í	A	T	Z	T	X	O	M	W
Q	S	S	F	R	O	M	T	D	T	I	K
P	T	V	X	B	K	P	M	P	O	G	T
Z	A	T	D	Y	P	Í	E	Z	P	O	R

Sopa de letras #31-40

Instrucciones: Busca cada una de las palabras de uso frecuente escondidas en esta sopa de letras. Las palabras aparecen horizontales o verticales. Usa un lápiz de color para colorear cada palabra.

estábamos	estaban	pero	él	qué
todos	allí	también	una	cuando

T	R	É	R	E	V	T	O	D	O	S	R
É	L	E	V	S	Z	N	C	B	O	W	P
T	P	H	U	T	W	D	Z	B	P	K	O
A	Í	A	L	Á	F	U	M	B	E	K	O
E	S	T	A	B	A	N	U	X	R	V	U
T	U	F	Q	A	B	U	T	V	O	S	R
A	K	W	É	M	Z	N	G	P	R	Q	Y
M	H	N	F	O	W	E	R	E	É	D	S
B	O	Q	Z	S	P	N	N	B	V	U	O
A	L	L	Í	T	A	M	B	I	É	N	V
C	D	W	J	T	B	Í	A	B	J	A	F
C	U	A	N	D	O	L	C	V	Q	U	É

Nombre: _____

Sopa de letras #41-50

Instrucciones: Busca cada una de las palabras de uso frecuente escondidas en esta sopa de letras. Las palabras aparecen horizontales o verticales. Usa un lápiz de color para colorear cada palabra.

| nos | de | dijo | mismo | me |
| cuál | los | te | al | junto |

S	Á	M	D	E	Y	Z	E	L	O	S	D
V	D	I	Z	B	Á	F	Q	S	R	K	T
U	K	S	N	Á	B	O	U	T	Á	D	P
X	G	M	E	V	O	E	L	W	R	T	E
Q	N	O	Q	T	Y	X	L	T	U	J	J
Á	I	L	L	U	H	O	W	Á	D	C	I
I	R	X	S	M	J	V	B	U	Z	U	B
I	F	H	R	Z	U	J	B	G	F	Á	Y
N	S	Á	U	P	N	K	T	B	U	L	O
W	H	I	C	H	T	C	O	R	N	S	O
I	K	N	O	S	O	C	E	A	C	H	R
T	H	D	I	J	O	Q	Q	L	A	U	R

71

Sopa de letras #51-60

Instrucciones: Busca cada una de las palabras de uso frecuente escondidas en esta sopa de letras. Las palabras aparecen horizontales o verticales. Usa un lápiz de color para colorear cada palabra.

muchas	algunas	otras	las	sus
éstas	ellas	afuera	ella	mucho

E	L	L	A	É	L	A	S	A	C	J	V
B	W	F	B	I	L	G	X	B	K	S	Q
T	M	U	C	H	A	S	N	M	P	U	F
F	T	W	M	U	C	H	O	J	É	S	I
P	J	F	M	D	H	D	O	T	R	A	S
M	É	S	T	A	S	Y	J	F	A	Z	B
J	I	K	T	H	É	M	D	U	L	U	W
T	G	I	L	D	R	T	P	H	G	N	W
S	E	A	I	O	U	T	L	P	U	H	Q
J	I	K	Y	W	N	O	T	H	N	R	V
V	J	S	P	E	L	L	A	S	A	O	É
A	F	U	E	R	A	H	Z	S	S	B	Y

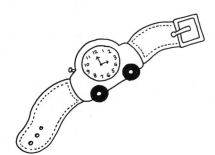

Sopa de letras #61-70

Instrucciones: Busca cada una de las palabras de uso frecuente escondidas en esta sopa de letras. Las palabras aparecen horizontales o verticales. Usa un lápiz de color para colorear cada palabra.

has	parece	dos	le	igual
dentro	tiene	más	hora	lo

C	Y	U	L	D	D	T	L	T	X	M	O
T	K	P	A	R	E	C	E	O	Q	B	W
I	I	M	S	W	N	D	S	Á	L	P	J
E	M	H	S	E	T	B	B	Y	I	E	T
N	M	E	E	O	R	Z	S	D	V	C	C
E	S	H	G	H	O	R	A	O	V	V	F
W	T	Q	M	A	A	S	A	S	Q	I	K
V	O	N	V	F	V	M	Á	S	W	G	Y
H	A	S	M	O	R	E	P	E	Q	U	E
H	E	R	O	Y	S	P	L	I	K	A	A
H	Á	F	M	G	Z	X	M	J	T	L	O
T	I	M	E	T	Á	B	D	Z	K	M	R

Sopa de letras #71-80

Instrucciones: Busca cada una de las palabras de uso frecuente escondidas en esta sopa de letras. Las palabras aparecen horizontales o verticales. Usa un lápiz de color para colorear cada palabra.

estoy	quién	primero	sé	antes
sin	mi	ahora	mejor	mis

A	É	P	S	S	É	L	S	I	N	F	P
H	R	O	W	Z	C	B	B	R	Z	P	R
O	S	T	Y	X	U	R	B	J	Y	O	I
R	F	I	R	S	É	Y	Q	Q	É	Q	M
A	A	K	A	S	S	C	O	L	G	P	E
O	A	N	N	W	Z	P	Q	B	C	Q	R
P	C	G	T	Y	X	S	C	G	W	Z	O
É	N	Z	E	B	T	H	Q	U	I	É	N
S	M	I	S	S	V	S	F	N	D	Y	V
L	J	E	S	T	O	Y	N	O	S	B	I
U	O	W	R	A	D	K	K	É	T	S	M
M	E	J	O	R	F	Z	S	N	S	B	I

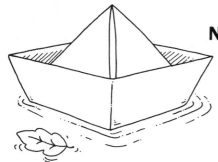

Sopa de letras #81-90

Instrucciones: Busca cada una de las palabras de uso frecuente escondidas en esta sopa de letras. Las palabras aparecen horizontales o verticales. Usa un lápiz de color para colorear cada palabra.

sola	usé	puedo	saber	sí
hice	sólo	aquí	si	agua

L	C	S	O	L	A	Y	C	Z	U	S	É
D	Í	D	N	Y	C	A	Q	U	Í	C	M
D	R	A	G	P	M	S	A	B	E	R	O
S	Í	N	D	B	G	M	S	F	W	N	U
A	Q	B	U	V	N	C	D	P	J	N	Y
D	X	O	V	E	R	W	X	P	X	Q	R
Í	E	U	W	N	J	U	G	F	W	U	S
H	B	N	J	U	S	K	S	I	M	N	P
Q	D	Ó	W	N	Ó	M	P	H	Q	P	H
E	S	T	B	H	G	C	Z	G	B	U	I
U	G	A	G	U	A	R	B	F	M	A	C
P	U	E	D	O	E	S	Ó	L	O	S	E

Nombre: _____

Sopa de letras #91-100

Instrucciones: Busca cada una de las palabras de uso frecuente escondidas en esta sopa de letras. Las palabras aparecen horizontales o verticales. Usa un lápiz de color para colorear cada palabra.

palabras	mayoría	largas	y	unos
sabes	muy	pocas	cortas	murciélago

O	I	Y	Z	Q	J	T	S	A	B	E	S
C	O	R	T	A	S	W	V	F	G	P	Y
L	É	S	T	X	C	U	N	O	S	P	H
A	B	L	G	O	T	D	X	Y	P	B	É
R	N	F	G	U	P	A	L	A	J	Q	L
G	F	W	C	W	O	R	D	S	L	S	X
A	Y	Q	C	T	M	M	O	S	T	B	B
S	N	O	P	A	L	A	B	R	A	S	T
F	U	W	R	K	É	Z	W	M	U	Y	É
C	P	O	C	A	S	J	N	T	X	C	R
M	U	R	C	I	É	L	A	G	O	M	Í
V	E	M	A	Y	O	R	Í	A	H	F	P

76

Tarjetas divertidas
#1-10

el	ese
es	un
con	está
a	tu
en	sobre

Tarjetas divertidas
#11-20

este	como
la	su
están	para
arriba	abajo
hay	ellos

Tarjetas divertidas
#21-30

yo	tenía
se	por
tengo	esta
no	ni
estar	conmigo

Tarjetas divertidas
#31-40

estábamos	todos
estaban	allí
pero	también
él	una
qué	cuando

nos	cuál
de	los
dijo	te
mismo	al
me	junto

corta por la línea más gruesa

muchas	éstas
algunas	ellas
otras	afuera
las	ella
sus	mucho

has	dentro
parece	tiene
dos	más
le	hora
igual	lo

corta por la línea más gruesa

estoy

sin

quién

mi

primero

ahora

sé

mejor

antes

mis

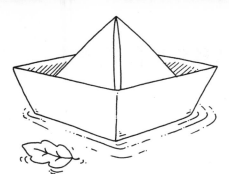

Tarjetas divertidas
#81-90

sola	hice
usé	sólo
puedo	aquí
saber	si
sí	agua

palabras	sabes
mayoría	muy
largas	pocas
y	cortas
unos	murciélago

Tarjetas divertidas
(en blanco)

Instrumento de evaluación estratégica

Student: _____ Grade: _____ Teacher: _____ Year: _____

Sight Word	Baseline Date	Date	Date	Date
1. el				
2. ese				
3. es				
4. un				
5. con				
6. está				
7. a				
8. tu				
9. en				
1o. sobre				
11. este				
12. como				
13. la				
14. su				
15. están				
16. para				
17. arriba				
18. abajo				
19. hay				
2o. ellos				
21. yo				
22. tenía				
23. se				
24. por				
25. tengo				
SCORE	/25	/25	/25	/25

Sight Word	Baseline Date	Date	Date	Date
26. esta				
27. no				
28. ni				
29. estar				
30. conmigo				
31. estábamos				
32. todos				
33. estaban				
34. allí				
35. pero				
36. también				
37. él				
38. una				
39. qué				
4o. cuando				
41. nos				
42. cuál				
43. de				
44. los				
45. dijo				
46. te				
47. mismo				
48. al				
49. me				
5o. junto				
SCORE	/25	/25	/25	/25

Sight Word	Baseline Date	Date	Date	Date
51. muchas				
52. éstas				
53. algunas				
54. ellas				
55. otras				
56. afuera				
57. las				
58. ella				
59. sus				
60. mucho				
61. has				
62. dentro				
63. parece				
64. tiene				
65. dos				
66. más				
67. le				
68. hora				
69. igual				
7o. lo				
71. estoy				
72. sin				
73. quién				
74. mi				
75. primero				
SCORE	/25	/25	/25	/25

Sight Word	Baseline Date	Date	Date	Date
76. ahora				
77. sé				
78. mejor				
79. antes				
80. mis				
81. sola				
82. hice				
83. usé				
84. sólo				
85. puedo				
86. aquí				
87. saber				
88. si				
89. sí				
90. agua				
91. palabras				
92. sabes				
93. mayoría				
94. muy				
95. largas				
96. pocas				
97. y				
98. cortas				
99. unos				
100. murciélago				
SCORE	/25	/25	/25	/25
TOTAL SCORE	/100	/100	/100	/100

Querida familia,

Les agradecemos que apoyen el aprendizaje del salón de clases practicando con sus hijos las Tarjetas de Lectura y Ortografía que aquí incluimos. Puesto que las palabras de uso frecuente son las que más a menudo los niños encuentran en su lectura, aprenderlas es la llave para que alcancen el éxito como lectores.

Pida a su hijo/a que corte las tarjetas divertidas y las guarde en una bolsa. Motívelo a consultarlas con frecuencia. A fin de reforzar la ortografía de las palabras, haga que su hijo/a lea la palabra, luego que dé vuelta a la tarjeta y escriba la palabra de memoria. Trabajen juntos, revisando si la ortografía está correcta. Si en la tarjeta de palabras la "L" está encerrada en un círculo, su hijo/a necesita aprender a leer la palabra. Si la letra "O" está encerrada en un círculo, su hijo/a necesita aprender la ortografía de la palabra.

Muchas gracias por su colaboración.

Tarjetas de Lectura y Ortografía

Instrucciones: Si la "L" va encerrada en un círculo, debes repasar la lectura de la palabra. Si la "O" está encerrada en un círculo debes repasar, la ortografía. Recorta las tarjetas divertidas y guárdalas en una bolsa. Debes consultarlas con frecuencia.

- Lee la palabra
- Da vuelta a la tarjeta y escribe la palabra.
- Verifica que la ortografía esté correcta.

L	O	L	O
L	O	L	O
L	O	L	O
L	O	L	O
L	O	L	O

Celebrate Achievement

To keep students engaged in the process of learning sight words, reward effort and achievement. If you like, use the ideas below to help make learning sight words a fun endeavor.

Try these fun ideas!

First 100 Words Party: As soon as the class has cumulatively mastered 100 words, have a party. When they master another 100 words, have another party!

BINGO Fest: Eat cupcakes! Drink juice! And play sight-word BINGO!

Sight-Word-of-the-Day: Write the word on a corner of your chalkboard. Ask students to look for the word as they do shared reading. As soon as children spot a sight word, they must raise their hands briefly. When every child has spotted at least one sight word it's time to celebrate. Invite the children to raise their hands above their heads and shout, "Hip Hip Hooray! We Read Sight Words Today!" You may also use this fun activity as a diagnostic tool. Some children may recognize sight words but cannot yet read them, so look to see which hands go up.

Certificates of Achievement: After each child learns yet another ten sight words, provide him/her with a certificate. Promote student self-confidence and literacy!

How to Use Sight-Word Certificates

By inviting students to decorate their very own certificates, you provide them with an opportunity to recognize and internalize their growing abilities.

- Supply students with copies of the certificate on page 92.
- Ask students to write the sight words they can spell on the certificate.
- Invite students to decorate certificates with markers, glued-on glitter, and stickers.
- Students may share the completed certificates with each other and family members.

Diploma
de
logros

entregado a

Mira cuántas palabras frecuentes has aprendido a leer y escribir.
Ya vas por el camino de la lectura y la escritura. ¡Felicitaciones!

Teacher

Date

la

su

el

ese

como

este

sobre

en

tu

a

está

con

un

es

Respuestas para Sopa de letras

Sopa de letras #1-10

```
A L S O B R E Y R H E S
O Y O U S G O M Y R T Q
L U T N F Q X P X N M L
X Y T P E G F S Y Á B Q
A O O R S Z D P B E R E
U Q K L E R E M N U X N
D I Z J D O F V T X Q Q
N T T Y M J C X V L C W
T Á S B K Y O E F D P D
Q P R T A N N X T R Á T
I N R H V J Z U F E L E
E S T Á J T U E H D F Z
```

Sopa de letras #11-20

```
E S T Á N Y C D O U X H
Á U W V K O R L P A R A
P H D F P M J F M R Y Y
Z G O N N G X M I N O I
J E L L O S U Q R H T B
S W T H E E L L M S V Q
H E O P S H A R R I B A
W E L U T L B N H B C B
N Q B J E W W Á S I G A
B Z E F O R B F H Á S J
L C G D F O E Q C L T O
A I T H B C O M O S W O
```

Sopa de letras #21-30

```
G E S T A R Z H E J H Y
H A V E G G Q Í P H S Í
S A S Q D S J N W P M A
N O J H A Y T E N G O S
H U V S H O K C K C R E
R R T O N E X T O G C G
T Z M F I P J M Z J O F
T L Í S Q O D Y L Q N R
T E N Í A T Z T X O M W
Q S S F R O M T D T I K
P T V X B K P M P O G T
Z A T D Y P Í E Z P O R
```

Sopa de letras #31-40

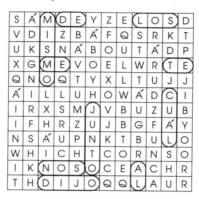

```
T R É R E V T O D O S R
É L E V S Z N C B O W P
T P H U T W D Z B P K O
A Í A L Á F U M B E K O
E S T A B A N U X R V U
T U F Q A B U T V O S R
A K W É M Z N G P R Q Y
M H N F O W E R E E D S
B O Q Z S P N N B V U O
A L L Í T A M B I É N V
C D W J T B Í A B J A F
C U A N D O L C V Q U É
```

Sopa de letras #41-50

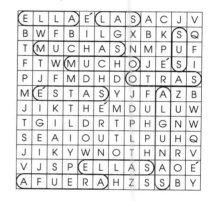

```
S Á M D E Y Z E L O S D
V D I Z B Á F Q S R K T
U K S N Á B O U T Á D P
X G M E V O E L W R T E
Q N O Q T Y X L T U J J
Á I L L U H O W Á D C I
I R X S M J V B U Z U B
I F H R Z U J B G F Á Y
N S Á U P N K T B U L O
W H I C H T C O R N S O
I K N O S O C E A C H R
T H D I J O Q Q L A U R
```

Sopa de letras #51-60

```
E L L A É L A S A C J V
B W F B I L G X B K S Q
T M U C H A S N M P U F
F T W M U C H O J E S I
P J F M D H D O T R A S
M É S T A S Y J F A Z B
J I K T H É M D U L U W
T G I L D R T P H G N W
S E A I O U T L P U H Q
J I K Y W N O T H N R V
V J S P E L L A S A O É
A F U E R A H Z S S B Y
```

Sopa de letras #61-70

```
C Y U L D D T L T X M O
T K P A R E C E O Q B W
I I M S W N D S Á L P J
E M H S E T B B Y I E T
N M E E O R Z S D V C C
E S H G H O R A O V V F
W T Q M A A S A S Q I K
V O N V F V M Á S W G Y
H A S M O R E P E Q U E
H E R O Y S P L I K A A
H Á F M G Z X M J T L O
T I M E T Á B D Z K M R
```

Sopa de letras #71-80

```
A É P S S E L S I N F P
H R O W Z C B B R Z P R
O S T Y X U R B J Y O I
R F I R S É Y Q Q É Q M
A A K A S S C O L G P E
O A N N W Z P Q B C Q R
P C G T Y X S C G W Z O
É N Z E B T H Q U I É N
S M I S S V S F N D Y V
L J E S T O Y N O S B I
U O W R A D K K É T S M
M E J O R F Z S N S B I
```

Sopa de letras #81-90

```
L C S O L A Y C Z U S É
D Í D N Y C A Q U Í C M
D R A G P M S A B E R O
S Í N D B G M S F W N U
A Q B U V N C D P J N Y
D X O V E R W X P X Q R
Í E U W N J U G F W U S
H B N J U S K S I M N P
Q D Ó W N Ó M P H Q P H
E S T B H G C Z G B U I
U G A G U A R B F M A C
P U E D O E S Ó L O S E
```

Sopa de letras #91-100

```
O I Y Z Q J T S A B E S
C O R T A S W V F G P Y
L É S T X C U N O S P H
A B L G O T D X Y P B É
R N F G U P A L A J Q L
G F W C W O R D S L S X
A Y Q C T M M O S T B B
S N O P A L A B R A S T
F U W R K É Z W M U Y É
C P O C A S J N T X C R
M U R C I É L A G O M Í
V E M A Y O R Í A H F P
```

93

Notas

Notas

Notas